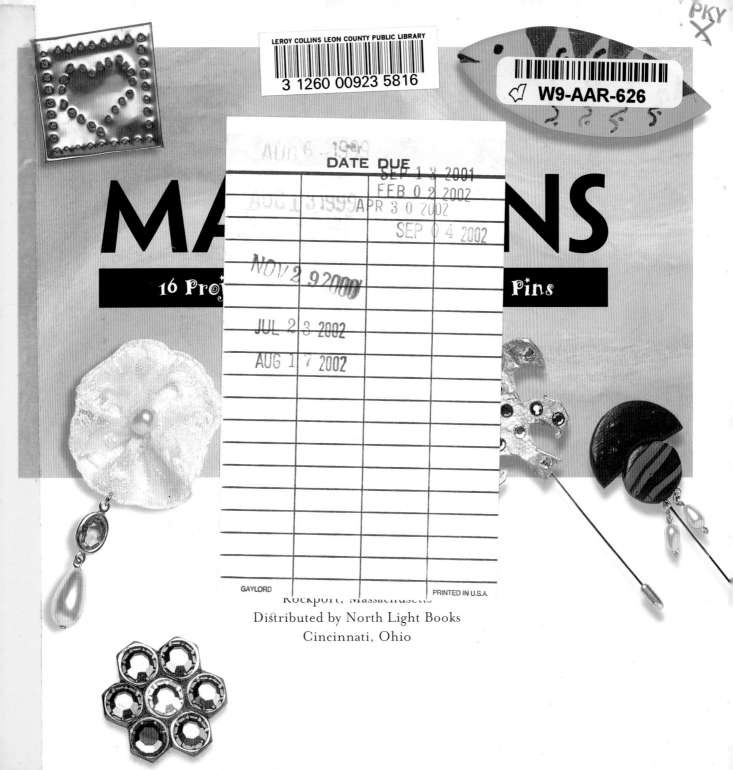

MA NS

16 Pro Pins

Rockport, Massachusetts
Distributed by North Light Books
Cincinnati, Ohio

First published in the United States of America by
Quarry Books, an imprint of Rockport Publishers, Inc.
146 Granite Street
Rockport, Massachusetts 01966-1299
Telephone: (508) 546-9590
Fax: (508) 546-7141

Distributed to the book trade and art trade
in the United States of America by
North Light, an imprint of F & W Publications
1507 Dana Avenue
Cincinnati, Ohio 45207
Telephone: (800) 289-0963

Other distribution by
Rockport Publishers, Inc.
Rockport, Massachusetts 01966-1299

ISBN: 1-56496-274-1

10   9   8   7   6   5   4   3   2   1

Designer: Laura Herrmann Design
Photography: Paul Forrester

Printed in Hong Kong
by Regent Publishing Services Limited

CONTENTS

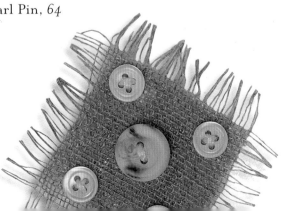

PIN BASICS

Y OU DON'T HAVE TO BE A HIGHLY SKILLED PROFESSIONAL TO CREATE beautiful pins that make you the envy of your friends. With just a little imagination and the right materials and tools, you can produce wonderful works of art from classic jewelry elements such as beads, precious metals, and stones. Or you can transform mundane, household items such as candy wrappers, fabric scraps, and newspapers into sophisticated pins. To produce fabulous designs with a professional finish, you will need the findings, tools, and techniques that join, link, and make up your pins.

Materials

Of all the materials available to be used in making pins, synthetic polymer clays are one of the most versatile. They can be used to make the most spectacular beads and bases for pins in every shape and size imaginable.

Fired in a domestic oven at a low temperature and then varnished, polymer clays can imitate some of the finest ceramics. They come in a fantastic range of colors that can be used alone, twisted together in various color combinations to create wonderful marbled effects, or built up into imitation millefiori canes for pin bases or charm drops.

Paper is suitable for any form of craft work and jewelry design is no exception. Use papier-mâché techniques to cover simple cardboard base shapes with newspaper to make stylish pins. Take advantage of the wide selection of decorative paper available and add a patterned finishing layer to a plain papier-mâché base. Roll colorful paper into bead charms to hang from a pin base or glue to a cardboard base in the shape of a stylized flower.

Beads, a basic component in making necklaces, bracelets, and earrings, can also be used to make striking pins. With a ball of plasticine as the base, make papier-mâché beads that can be decorated in your own style or painted to mimic real beads.

Pick up other materials at yard sales and antique fairs—dismantled old watches make novel pin bases, and their cogs and wheels can be hung as charms. Never throw out a broken necklace or bracelet—the remaining beads and clasps can always be worked into new designs.

Almost all jewelry making requires the use of *findings,* which is the jeweler's term for the basic components that give your design a neat finish. Findings help each piece hang correctly. They should be the right size for your pin; if they are in proportion to the materials that you choose, they will help balance the overall design.

PIN BACKS are essential for a professional finish and come in a choice of metal finishes. Flat bar backs, the most versatile kind of pin back, have pierced holes along their length. They can be glued or sewn to the reverse side of your design. The holes also allow you to sew beads directly to the back. Pin backs come in different lengths but are generally the same width. They are available in flat metal shapes, usually circular or oval with a pin fastening already soldered in place. These look wonderful with cabochons glued directly to them. Larger backs are perfect for supporting polymer clay and papier-mâché shapes. You can buy special perforated fittings with claws that clamp over a corresponding base and these can be used to sew beads or fabric designs to.

STICK PINS come in a variety of lengths to be made into hat or lapel pins. They have a blunt head and pointed end that should be inserted into a protective cap. Other variations come with a flat disc set at the top to glue to a variety of beads or bases.

JUMP RINGS are circular or oval metal rings that are not completely joined together. They come in a variety of sizes and thicknesses to suit all kinds of jewelry projects. Use them to link two findings together.

Other Findings

HEAD PINS and EYE PINS are wire pins that come in varying lengths. A head pin is like a blunt-ended dressmaker's pin that is particularly useful for making charms. Eye pins have a preformed loop at one end and are most often used to link beads or findings together but can also be used to make beaded bar pins.

JEWELER'S WIRE is available in gold, silver, and copper or plated metals and in several different gauges. You can use wire to make your own hat and lapel pins by using a metal file to sharpen the ends into a point. Wire is also easy to coil and work into intricate shapes and decorative spirals. The finer the gauge, the easier it is to work with, but choose a thickness to suit the beads and the overall design, especially if using it for making stick pins. Wire is also useful when head and eye pins are not long enough or are too thick to pass through tiny beads.

Other useful findings for making pins are ornate END SPACERS and HANGERS, which often have two, three, or five preformed holes on one side and a single loop on the other. With a little creativity they can be decorated with charms and linked to a flat bar back. Pretty PENDANT CLASPS can be used at the top of bead charms and linked with jump rings to your design. These ensure that the charm hangs correctly and can be used to clamp directly on to more unusual fabric or seed charms.

The most important findings for pin making are the pin backs themselves, plus jump rings and head or eye pins. These may all sound rather strange now but by the time you have worked through the projects in this book, they will be much more familiar to you. All findings are readily available in craft stores, from bead suppliers, and even in department stores. You can buy them in precious or nonprecious metals.

Tools & Adhesives

All of the projects in this book are easy to make and require little space for their creation—most can be put together at the kitchen table with only the basic tools. Lay down a craft board to protect the table from damage, and provide a flat, even surface to work on. A self-healing cutting mat, marked with ruled lines, makes it easy to draw and cut shapes.

Small round-nosed and needle-nosed pliers, available at jewelry and bead suppliers, make opening, closing, and linking together findings much easier. Use round-nosed pliers to turn loops, and to twist and coil wire into shape. Squeeze calotte crimps together and flatten

joints with needle-nosed pliers.

Use two pairs of pliers to open and close jump rings. Buy them with integral wire cutters or invest in a separate pair of wire cutters for trimming head and eye pins, and jeweler's wire.

As a general rule, an all-purpose, clear-drying glue and a stronger, bonding epoxy glue are all you will need to ensure that your wonderful design won't break when you wear it. Take the time to read and follow the directions on the glue container. Use common sense: make sure that bead and finding surfaces are clean and grease-free; and, with some glues, you may need to work in a well-ventilated room.

Linking Beads

Groups of beads, whether in several shades of the same color or bright clashing colors, look wonderful wired with head or eye pins and linked together to make bar pins or pretty charms to dangle from your design. You can wire each bead individually, which is quite time-consuming but produces an expensive-looking finish, or work the beads in small groups.

To make charm drops, use a head pin, a particularly useful finding for making drops because the flat head prevents beads from sliding off the pin. If the head pin slips through the bead hole, add a small stopper bead first. Slide the beads onto the pin in the order you want, trim the wire with wire cutters if necessary, and then turn a loop with round-nosed pliers. The loop can then be attached to a pin finding or a jump ring.

Eye pins are ideal for linking beads together and for attaching charms to pin base shapes because they already have a preformed loop in one end.

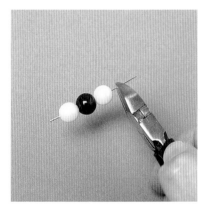

Trimming a head pin already threaded with beads.

Use short pins to hang single beads from pin bases and longer ones for groups of beads. Slide the beads onto each pin, trim the wire, and turn a loop, just as you would with a head pin. To link the beads together, use jump rings or open up a loop on the pin and join to the next loop. Make

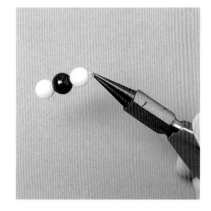

Turning a loop on the head pin.

sure you close the loops securely or they will come undone when you wear them.

You can also substitute jeweler's wire for the head and eye pins. To make charm drops, you will need to turn a small spiral in the end with round-nosed pliers. You can then leave this protruding as a decorative effect or turn it under so the bottom bead sits on it. For linking beads and making insertion pins, simply turn a loop in each end with pliers.

Making Simple Pin Bases

Flat-backed pins are easy to make from polymer and air-dry clays, papier-mâché shapes, and fabric that can be decorated with colorful paint effects, dazzling bead charms, or delicate embroidery.

The simplest bases can be shaped from polymer clays that come in a wide range of colors to use on their own or mixed together to create marbled or millefiori effects. Knead the clay for several minutes to soften and smooth, then roll out flat, like pastry, to a thickness of about ¼ to ⅜ inch / .6 to 1 cm. Make sure the clay is the same depth all over, then simply cut out the shape you require. If you don't like the results, just roll up the clay, knead until smooth, and start again. Use cookie cutters, a cardboard template shaped to your own design, or natural elements like fallen leaves to create your own clay shapes. Layer shapes on top of one another to create a three-dimensional look and give them a textured finish by pressing anything from a cheese grater to the end of a plastic drinking straw onto the surface. For a glittering jewel-encrusted finish, press glass beads and flat-backed jewel stones into the surface—they must be glass or they will melt when you bake the piece. Simple pin base shapes such as lizards, dragonflies, and bows, inspired by marcasite-studded animal pins of the 1930s, are easy to recreate in clay.

Layer cardboard shapes with pasted strips of newspaper to make another simple pin base that

can be painted and decorated in endless ways. Add texture by gluing string in a pretty pattern to the base before layering, then affix jewel stones to the finished painted design. Look in history books for such design ideas and shapes as a Celtic shield, or create abstract shapes for a contemporary design.

All these basic forms can be animated with bead charms and drops by inserting eye pins or piercing holes at the relevant points in the pin base. Dangle a single beautiful jewel or several beaded strands from the center bottom of the design. Insert an eye pin trimmed to size (about ¼ to ⅜ inch / .6 to 1 cm, depending on the size of the design) into the edge of the clay design

before baking and, once the clay has set hard, add a dab of glue to secure it. Join wired single beads or groups of beads directly or with a jump ring to the eye pin.

Decorative necklace clasps can also be turned into instant pins by separating the two parts, discarding the plain section, and gluing a pin back to the reverse side. These are often very ornate and can be set with pearls, jewel stones, and diamanté. Use the attached loop to hang stunning beads or other charms. Necklace clasps are not the only unusual idea for pin bases. You can also adapt large flat, doughnut-style beads typically used as pendants. By looking past the obvious, you can find all sorts of ingenious alternatives.

Finishing Techniques

How you finish a pin can make or break your design. To get a truly professional look, use findings—the tiny metal components used to link, join, and complete a design. Jump rings join findings and groups of beads or charms to the design. To keep the shape of the ring, and to ensure that the two ends meet perfectly again,

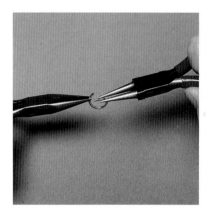

Hold a jump ring with two pairs of pliers positioned at either side of the joint. Gently twist the ends away from each other sideways to open, and twist back again to close.

open the rings at the joint using pliers (two pairs of pliers are ideal), twisting the ends away from each other sideways rather than just pulling them apart. To close, simply twist the ends back again so that they meet exactly. Practice opening and closing them before starting your project.

Calotte crimps, though used more often for making necklaces and bracelets, disguise ugly end knots on nylon or cotton thread or tiger tail used to hang bead charms from a pin base. The preformed loop on the base can be joined to a jump ring or directly to the design.

Round calottes look like tiny metal beads when they are closed. They are hinged either at the side or bottom and have a gap for the thread to pass through. For sideways-opening calottes,

Place the knot at the end of a length of thread in the cup of a calotte crimp and squeeze the two halves together using needle-nosed pliers.

position the knot in the "cup" of one half and use needle-nosed pliers to squeeze the two sides together. Make sure the thread is going in the right direction before you secure the crimp. If you are using calottes that open from the loop end, you will need to pass the thread through a small gap in the hinged end before knotting, then close in the same way as before. Use square calottes for thick cord or thong; they are open on one side, which is where you insert the thread. With needle-nosed pliers, fold one side over the thread and then the other side to secure the thread. An alternative is crimp beads, tiny metal beads, that hold loops in the ends of nylon line or tiger tail. Simply thread them into position and squeeze firmly with pliers to secure.

To finish a basic pin, make sure the bar or disc back is the right size to support the design and is positioned in the correct place to ensure the pin sits correctly or it will fall forward

when worn. It is easy to check this by temporarily fixing the finding in place with Blu Tak or plasticine. Use long stick pins for hat pins and shorter ones for lapel pins. If you can't find the right length, make your own stick pins from jeweler's wire—file a point at one end with a metal file and make a protective cap from a tiny pressed cotton ball painted to match the design or a bead with its hole filled with a scrap of neoprene or rubber.

You can make your own stick pin from heavy-gauge jeweler's wire by filing a point at one end with a metal file.

BEAD IDEAS

A VISIT TO YOUR LOCAL CRAFTS STORE will reveal an array of beads to use in making your pin designs. Or be adventurous and create your own beads with paper, colorful synthetic clays, or even fabric.

Clay Beads

One of the most versatile materials to use is polymer clay. It is available in a fantastic range of colors, molds easily, and sets hard in a low-temperature oven. There are several comparable brands available, each with their own malleability, baking time, and color selection. The following basic techniques explain how to make clay beads for charm drops or for beads on hat and lapel pins. You can also apply these guidelines to making flat pin bases by rolling the clay out like pastry on a flat surface and cutting out the shapes with a craft knife or shaped cookie cutters. To attach beads to a hat or lapel pin, insert wire or trimmed eye pins in the clay before baking. It is a good idea to secure these findings with a dab of glue after the clay has hardened.

Plain beads and pin bases in a single color can be molded into any shape you want and then decorated with acrylic paints (watercolor paints don't cover as well). To make the beads, first knead the clay until it is soft and pliable, then roll it out into a log shape, ¼ to ¾ inch / .5 to 2 cm in diameter, depending on how big you want the bead to be.

For tube beads, cut the log into equal lengths and pierce the center with a toothpick or knitting needle. Pierce the bead from both ends to get neat holes; if you just push the stick straight through, make sure that you smooth the rough edges where the stick emerges. Round beads are made in the same way but each piece of clay is shaped into a ball in the palms of your hands. Pierce holes with a toothpick as above. Square beads are also made from a long log that is then flattened into a square against the edge of a knife or piece of wood. Cut to size and pierce as before. Add texture and detail to plain beads of any shape by pressing modeling tools, coins, and so on, against the surface, or by adding small strips or dots of other colors.

Experiment with several colors for more exciting finishes, such as marbling or millefiori. To create a marbled effect, roll out logs of two or more colors and wrap them around each other. Knead these together, roll them back into a larger log, folding it in half and twisting until the colors are blended. Be careful not to knead too much or the individual colors will disappear and the clay will eventually return to a new, single color. Shape beads as described above.

Millefiori, or "thousand flower" beads, are slightly more complicated, but rewarding to make once you have mastered the techniques. Begin with a core color—either a plain log or two colors rolled together. Then place other logs in different colors around the core, completely surrounding it. The colors are usually placed in a regular pattern and must be gently pressed together to ensure no air is trapped inside. The whole cane is then wrapped in another sheet of clay, carefully rolled out to a diameter of about ¼ inch / .5 cm, and cut into tiny slices that are pressed on an unbaked base bead to cover it.

Safety Note

Always read the instructions given on the polymer clay package. This clay gives off fumes, especially as it bakes, and should be used in a well-ventilated room.

Bead Ideas **15**

Paper Beads

Using paper is one of the easiest and cheapest ways to make beads and pin bases. Use paper beads to decorate hat and lapel pins or glue them to a thick cardboard base shape to make attractive flat pins. Traditional round beads look pretty glued in a flower shape with one bead in the center surrounded by a ring of other beads; conical rolled paper beads can radiate out from a jewel-stone center on a disc of cardboard or place them side-by-side in a row on an oblong of piece of cardboard. To make an instant pin, glue a pin back to one side of an oversized rolled bead.

The simplest papier-mâché beads can be made by shaping pieces of newspaper into a ball and then layering pasted strips of newspaper over it. For a smoother finish, layer the paper strips over a ball of plasticine. When the ball is completely dry, cut it in half with a craft knife and remove the plasticine to lighten the paper beads. Glue the two halves of the bead back together and conceal the joint with another layer of paper before decorating.

To make rolled paper beads, use wrapping paper or magazines, or paint your own designs onto plain paper; cut into strips or elongated triangles, and roll up tightly around a toothpick. To give the beads a glossy, durable finish, paint them with clear nail polish.

Fabric Beads

You can use fabric to make all kinds of beads that can be decorated with embroidery or sewn stitches, or even with tiny beads. To make little puffs of fabric, cut the fabric out in circles, hem the edges, and draw up the edges. Puff beads make great fabric pins joined to a bar finding or hat or lapel pins. For tube beads, strips of fabric can be joined and gathered at either end. To give them shape, wrap them over a cardboard base or stuff with a little padding.

Wooden Beads & Pressed Cotton Beads

Most craft suppliers stock unvarnished wooden beads and pressed cotton balls in a variety of sizes. These are both easy to paint and decorate in you own individual style. Support the beads on wooden skewers, tops of pencils, or old paintbrush handles while painting, and leave to dry on a knitting needle stuck in a block of plasticine or polystyrene. Keep patterns simple. If you want to use several colors, let each color dry before starting the next. When you are finished, protect the surface with a coat of clear varnish or nail polish.

Miscellaneous Bead Ideas

Roll ordinary kitchen foil or colored candy foil wrappers to make bead shapes. Pierce the center with a sharp needle and, to make a charm, thread the bead onto a head or eye pin. Or add colored foil as a decorative final layer on a papier-mâché bead. Salt dough, which needs to bake in a low-temperature oven for several hours, is another good medium for making beads of different shapes. Both foil and clay can be painted and decorated to suit your design.

Pasta, seeds, nuts, and even washers can be painted, decorated, and used to make spectacular pins—no one will ever guess their origins. Use your imagination, and you will discover that all sorts of bits and pieces—safety pins, colorful paper clips, and even rubber bands can be turned into jewelry.

CREATING A DESIGN

Finding Inspiration

THE STARTING POINT IN ANY DESIGN IS FINDING INSPIRATION. Ideas for jewelry designs can come from a visit to a museum or a library. Look to the ancient Egyptian, Roman, and Celtic civilizations, as well as the more recent Arts and Crafts and Art Deco periods, for ideas. A walk in the country or along the seashore can put you in touch with one of the greatest and most economical design source libraries: Mother Nature. Flowers and foliage, rocks and minerals, insect and animal life all can spur the imagination. The sky provides us with the sun, moon, and star motifs that are perfect for interpreting into jewelry forms. The sea washes up shells on the beach and sculpts pebbles and wood into interesting shapes.

Don't forget the materials you have on hand. Beads and fabrics can fall accidentally and often haphazardly together to create striking and unusual combinations. Paints and decorative finishes are fun to experiment with. Clays can be molded into unusual shapes and given textured finishes.

Working Out a Design

Once you have found your inspiration, try to sketch out different ideas on paper. You will need a sketch book, tracing paper, pencils, colored crayons, felt tip markers (including gold and silver markers), an eraser, and a pencil sharpener. You don't have to draw works of art; rough sketches will suffice.

Work out the shape and size of the pin so that it is in proportion to where you wear it, then position extra details such as charm drops, beads, or jewel stones. Consider symmetry and balance as you design so that no one side appears strikingly different or out of proportion with the rest of the design. After working out your basic design, decide on the best type and size of pin fitting that will support the piece. Write down other findings you will need next to your design sketch. If you want to try unusual decorative effects or handpainted intricate designs, sketch or paint them on paper before attempting to make the real thing.

Write down the findings you will need next to your design sketch. If you want to try any unusual paint effects or create complex millefiori beads, experiment with paints on paper before moving on to a sample bead.

Badge-Style
PINS

P ins have been used in both functional and decorative forms for thousands of years. The ancient Greeks fastened the shoulders of their *peplos,* or outer garments, with open pins with decorated heads. These were later replaced by more substantial *fibulae,* or brooches.

Badge-style pins, one of the easiest pieces of jewelry to make, are still a great way of holding scarves in place or for dressing up a plain outfit. This style has no dangles and is turned into a pin by simply gluing or sewing a flat metal bar with a pin and catch to the back of a plain metal disc. Pin backs and plain metal discs are available from jewelry, bead, and craft suppliers. You can also buy perforated fittings with claws that will clamp over the metal base plates, making it easy to sew on ornate beads or decorative buttons.

Many kinds of materials—from traditional beads and jewel stones to craft rubber and sheet metals—can be added for exciting effects. Dazzling jewel stones set in mounts look wonderful glued together in the shape of a cross; ordinary metal hexagonal nuts fit

together to make a flower-shaped pin that looks sensational decorated with flat-backed jewels. Fine sheet metals like pewter, copper, and aluminum are easy to cut and shape with tin cutters or a craft knife and can be given a pierced Shaker design or a relief pattern taken from ancient artifacts.

Glittering Floral
FANTASY

Design Tips

Lay out the metal nuts and stones in their mounts on a flat surface and experiment with different shapes, making sure the sides of each stone or nut butt up against each other sufficiently to produce a solid finish when glued together.

Try painting metal nuts different colors with enamel paints and choose jewel stones to match. A shiny black base looks stunning set with crystal jewels or pearls for a traditional look, but you could experiment with brighter colors for a more contemporary feel.

Use mounts for jewel stones that are suitable for sewing, and try creating more exciting shapes by pushing wire through the ready-made holes to link the stones together.

Fill the holes in nuts with paper pulp to provide a base for textured paints, enamel paints, or glittering liquid jewels instead of jewel stones or beads.

NOTHING IS MORE REWARDING THAN TURNING something very ordinary into something spectacular, and this pin is a great example of what can be done with "found" objects. The base is made from simple metal nuts, the kind usually teamed with bolts for fixing things around the house. Their hexagonal shape means that they can be fitted together to make a pretty flower shape that looks sensational decorated with dazzling flat-backed jewels. The colors of the jewels can be chosen to match a particular outfit, and you can experiment with other styles of jewels and beads to create different effects. The metal nuts themselves can also be glued into a variety of different shapes. Be sure to use a substantial epoxy glue to ensure a durable product. Different stone shapes suit different styles: oblong cut crystals can easily be made into a glittering cross design, whereas oval and heart-shaped stones look better in floral-inspired shapes.

You Will Need

Cardboard
Epoxy glue and spatula
7 metal nuts
7 flat-backed jewel stones
Tweezers
Pin back

Getting Started

Choose flat-backed jewel stones that will completely cover the holes in the nuts. Use tweezers to better handle and position the small stones.

GLITTERING FLORAL FANTASY

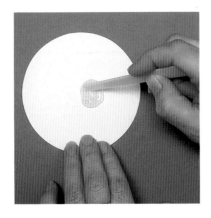

Squeeze a small amount of glue onto a piece of cardboard following the package instructions and mix thoroughly with the spatula supplied.

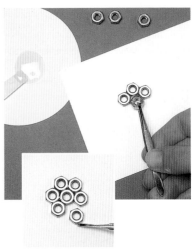

Glue the sides of the nuts together, beginning at the top of the design. Join the center nut. Continue gluing the nuts to each other until they are all in place and let dry according to the package instructions.

Glue the jewel stones in place, covering the holes in the nuts.

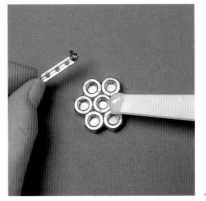

Glue the pin back in place just above center to make sure the pin doesn't fall forward with its own weight.

Variations on a Theme

FACETED CRYSTAL CROSS

The same principles can be applied to jewel stones that you can buy with special mounts designed for sewing or soldering in place.

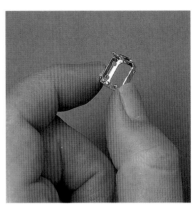

Position the stones centrally within the mount, making sure they are level and not slanting.

Use flat- or needle-nosed pliers to gently squeeze the claw over the stones to secure them.

Lay the stones out in the shape of a cross and glue the edges that butt against each other. When the glue has set, position a pin back across the horizontal bar of the cross.

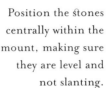

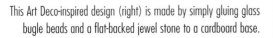

This Art Deco-inspired design (right) is made by simply gluing glass bugle beads and a flat-backed jewel stone to a cardboard base.

Linen & Button
SAMPLER

A SAMPLER BROOCH PROVIDES THE PERFECT BASE FOR displaying a collection of beautiful buttons or other precious objects. Its soft, flexible appearance is deceptive—it is in fact rigid and therefore more durable than an ordinary piece of fabric. Stiffening fabric is very easy and opens up a world of new ideas for using it as jewelry-making material. There are several ways to stiffen fabric, but one of the easiest is simply to apply a coat of clear-drying PVA glue. When dry, it leaves a transparent plastic-like coating on the fabric. Pleats, gathers, and folds can be made permanent, creating interesting sculptural effects. The basic idea can be applied to a wide range of fabrics from silk to lace and an infinite variety of shapes to suit your personal style, outfit, or occasion.

You Will Need

Piece of linen
Scissors
PVA glue
Paintbrush
Ceramic plate
Toothpick
Tailor's chalk
Selection of buttons
Coordinating embroidery thread
Small tapestry needle
All-purpose, clear-drying glue
Pin back

Getting Started

For this pin, you will need a piece of linen 1½ inches / 3.8 cm square. When gluing the fabric, turn it over several times while it is drying, or else it may stick to the plate and be pulled out of shape when removed.

LINEN & BUTTON SAMPLER

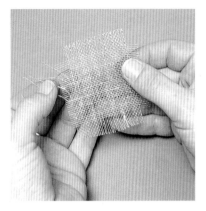

Carefully fray the edges of the linen square evenly all around to leave a central area of fabric approximately 1 inch / 2.5 cm square.

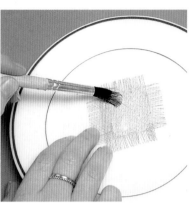
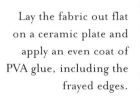

Lay the fabric out flat on a ceramic plate and apply an even coat of PVA glue, including the frayed edges.

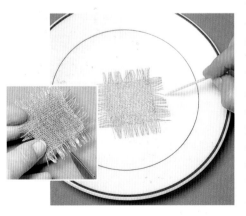

Use a toothpick to tease the frayed edges back into shape, then let dry. Turn the fabric over before it's completely dry to help prevent it from sticking to the plate. Use the tips of a pair of scissors to separate the frayed edges if necessary.

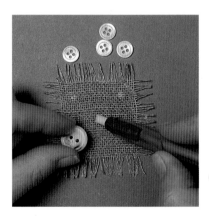

Lay the buttons on the fabric and work out your design. Mark their final positions with tailor's chalk.

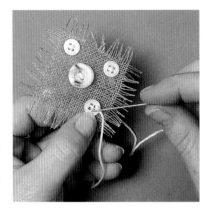

5. Sew each button in place securely with color-coordinated embroidery thread.

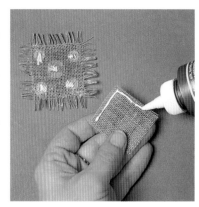

6. Cut out a square of linen, 1 inch / 2.5 cm, to use as a backing and glue it in place to cover any knots or ugly threads on the back of the sampler.

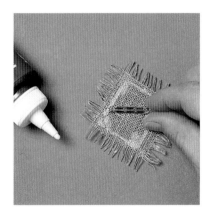

7. Glue a pin back in position and let dry completely.

Variations on a Theme

The stiffened fabric in this variation (right) has been used to create a sharper, more sophisticated shape. Tiny gold beads outline the heart and a decorative metal spiral adds the perfect finishing touch.

A pleated strip of dark blue silk, stiffened with PVA glue, is stitched at the base to make a fan shape, and then decorated with a diamanté trim and a dramatic jewel (far right).

Shaker-Style
PUNCHED TIN

WORKING WITH METAL CAN BE A DAUNTING thought for many people, since it is automatically assumed that technical skills and expensive equipment are needed. A great deal depends on the choice of metal, and the sheet pewter used for this project couldn't be easier to work with. It is a soft metal that's easily cut and shaped, just like fabric, using heavy-duty scissors or a craft knife. The inspiration for the pierced design comes from traditional punched tin work popular during the Shaker movement. Not only is it easy to master, but it provides scope for creating a wide variety of different motifs once you gain a little experience and get used to the feel of the metal. Pewter work is a popular craft on its own; many books and manuals illustrate the different techniques and will provide inspiration for more complicated designs.

Getting Started

You can use a pair of scissors to cut thin metal, but beware: the metal will blunt the cutting edge of the scissors. Try tin cutters to snip through thicker metals. For best results when cutting the metal, work on an old cutting board.

You Will Need

Small sheet of pewter
Cutting mat
Darning needle or bodkin
Steel ruler
Scissors
Craft knife
China marker
Small hammer
Panel pin
Piece of board
(an old bread board is ideal)
Pin back
Epoxy glue

SHAKER-STYLE PUNCHED TIN

1.

Place the metal sheet on top of a cutting mat and use the tip of the needle and a steel ruler to draw a square approximately 1½ inches / 4 cm, with a border of ¼ inch / 0.5 cm. Press firmly so that the metal is indented with the shape.

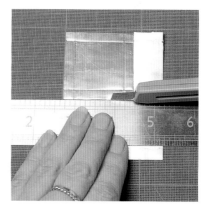

2.

Guide a craft knife along the edge of a steel ruler to cut along the border, making sure the ruler follows the marked lines.

3.

Cut across each corner at a 45° angle, using the tips of your scissors. Fold over the border edges along the indented lines to enclose the needle lines. Trim the corners to neaten if necessary.

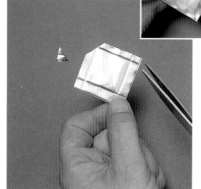

4.

Mark the border outline with the tip of a darning needle, making light indentations. Keep the lines straight by working along the edge of the steel ruler.

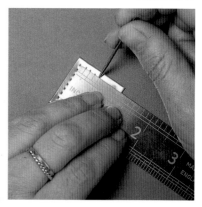

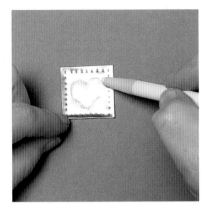

5. Using the china marker, draw a freehand heart in the center and mark the outline as before.

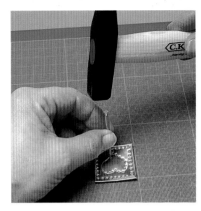

6. Working on a cutting mat on top of a piece of board, place the point of the panel pin over each indentation and hammer out the complete design, piercing the metal.

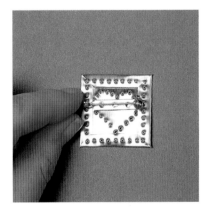

7. Glue the pin back in place and let dry completely.

Variations on a Theme

Copper is rich in color and is another soft metal that is easy to work with. The inspiration for this design (right) comes from an Art Nouveau–style quilting design and was drawn on the metal with a knitting needle over a traced motif.

This snake motif (far right) is an Aztec design reputedly representing a favored god.

Fun
FLOWERS

THE CRAFT FOAM RUBBER USED TO MAKE THESE FUN flower pins is called neoprene and has a delightful tactile finish that fascinates adults and children alike. It is a versatile medium that is easy to obtain from craft specialists and can be used for a wide variety of projects. You can buy it in sheets, just like cardboard or felt, in an inspiring range of colors from hot brights to cool pastels. Like felt, it is easy to transfer designs to, and it cuts like a dream with scissors or a craft knife, making it possible to achieve perfect detail with more intricate shapes. It can be used not only to make simple flat designs but also is flexible enough to be rolled, twisted, and curved into more interesting three-dimensional shapes. You can also buy the foam in craft packs of pre-cut shapes like the flowers, hearts, and circles used to make this project. Pinching the edge of a circle produces a simple petal shape, which then inspired the design for this fun pin.

Getting Started

For this pin, make sure that the larger precut circles are 1⅛ inches / 3 cm in diameter and that the smaller circle is ¾ inch / 2 cm in diameter. Once all the petals have been glued to the center, use a pair of tweezers to position and glue the central bead.

5 large yellow craft foam circles
1 small yellow craft foam circle
All-purpose, clear-drying glue
Clothespin
Pin back
Small black bead

FUN FLOWERS

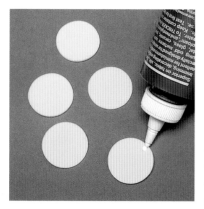

1.

Put a small blob of glue on each of the larger foam circles, close to the edge. Pinch the foam at the glued point to create a petal shape.

2.

Use a clothespin to hold the shape as the glue dries.

3.

Cover the smaller circle with glue and arrange the petals in a flower shape on top. Let dry completely.

4.

Glue a pin back in position.

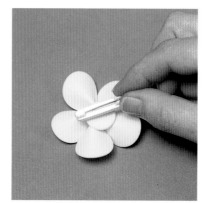

5.

Finish the flower by gluing a small black bead to the center point, between the petals.

PURPLE PASSION FLOWER

Cut out carefully with scissors or a craft knife.

1. Draw or trace 5 petal shapes onto craft rubber.

3. Apply glue to a contrasting-colored circle of foam and position the petals on top in the shape of a flower. Glue another circle of foam over the center and, when dry, complete with a pin back.

This black-eyed Susan is just one of the hundreds of ideas you can use craft rubber for (right).

Golden Celtic
SHIELD

I T IS NOT SURPRISING that papier-mâché (French for "mashed paper") is such a popular craft; its versatility and inexpensiveness, added to the fact that it requires so little space to work in, make it a great medium for lots of projects, especially in jewelry making. In the nineteenth century, papier-mâché was used to make tables and chairs, and these appear from time to time at auctions looking as good as new—which just goes to show how solid and sturdy the finished items are. One of the easiest papier-mâché techniques to master is layering pasted strips of torn paper over a base shape. You only need to ensure that the layers are smooth, with no air bubbles or lumps of paste (unless you want a textured finish). The design for this pin is influenced by a traditional Celtic shield. Small jewel stones complete the design and give it a touch of glamour.

Getting Started

Cut the piece of cardboard to a more manageable size before drawing the circle. Later, when you are ready to use the gold paint, lay the cardboard disc on a piece of scrap paper on top of newspaper to catch the extra paint.

You Will Need

Cardboard
Pencil
Compass
Scissors
Wallpaper paste
Paste brush
Small strips of torn newspaper
PVA glue
Gesso
Paintbrush
White acrylic enamel
Fine paintbrush
Gold metallic marker pen
4 small and 1 large
flat-backed jewel stones
Tweezers
Pin back
All-purpose, clear-drying glue

GOLDEN CELTIC SHIELD

1.

Using a compass and pencil, draw a circle, 2 inches / 5 cm in diameter, on the cardboard. Carefully cut out the circle using sharp scissors to get smooth edges.

2.

Paste strips of newspaper over the circle and smooth to cover both sides and the edges. You will need 4 to 6 layers in all to create a firm, finished piece, and the last 2 or 3 should be painted with PVA glue instead of paste to give a more durable finish. Let dry completely.

4.

Use the compass to lightly draw a narrow border in pencil.

3.

Paint with artist's gesso. This acts as an undercoat and prevents the newsprint from showing through the painted finish. When dry, paint with white acrylic enamel.

5.

Carefully paint the border gold with a metallic marker pen or with paint and a fine brush.

6.

Draw 2 inner circles, one smaller than the other, and paint as before. When dry, draw gold spokes radiating out from this inner circle.

7.

Glue a small jewel stone inside each of the 4 segments and a large stone to the center. Glue a pin back in place to complete.

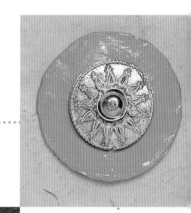

Variations on a Theme

This variation on the same theme experiments with textured glitter paints, creating a completely different look (right).

Painted a striking color and decorated with a charm recycled from a broken earring, this pin still shows the influence of the Celtic shield and is simple to make (far right).

Fantasy FISH

Design Tips

Sketch out your design ideas on paper and work out the scale and balance.

You can make a paste from a little air-dry clay mixed with water and brush it over the surface to fill in any cracks and create a smooth finish.

File rough edges with an emery board.

Like polymer clays, air-dry clays are easy to shape using the variety of cookie cutters available.

Children's arts and crafts books are a great resource for simple, stylized motifs that you can decorate with clever paint techniques and stylish color combinations.

Speed up drying time by placing the clay shape in a low-temperature oven. Experiment with test pieces of clay to find the right time and temperature.

THE DESIGN FOR THIS STYLIZED fish was inspired by the motif on a set of contemporary plates seen in a store. It was easy to re-create as a fun pin using air-dry clay as the base and adding the decorative details with special porcelain paints to make it look as if it was made of fine china. Keeping to a classic blue and white color combination added to the effect, but it would also look great painted in the bold, bright colors of exotic tropical fish. Modern air-dry clays produce a wonderful ceramic finish without the need for an expensive kiln and can be painted with acrylics, cold enamel, and ceramic paints as well as the porcelain paints used here. The clay is easy to mold, sculpt, and cut just like polymer clay and can be substituted for most of the projects that don't rely on the polymer clay colors.

You Will Need

Cardboard
Pencil
Ruler
Air-dry clay
Rolling pin
Craft knife
Emery board
White, light blue, and dark blue porcelain paints
Paintbrush
All-purpose, clear-drying glue
Pin back

Getting Started

To fill in cracks and even out rough surfaces in the clay, mix a little clay with water to form a smooth paste.

FANTASY FISH

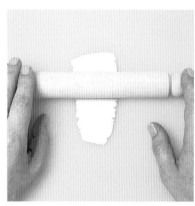

Roll out the clay to a depth of approximately ¼ inch / 0.5 cm.

Draw a template on the cardboard. To obtain the ellipse shape, use a ruler to draw a line the length of the finished pin—approximately 2½ inches / 6.5 cm. Mark the center point and 2 additional points ½ inch / 1 cm to each side. Draw a curved line from one end of the line up to the marked point and back to the other end of the line. Repeat on the other side and cut out the shape.

Place the cardboard template on top of the clay and use a craft knife to cut around it carefully. Smooth edges and any obvious cracks and let dry until completely hard. Use an emery board to file any remaining rough edges.

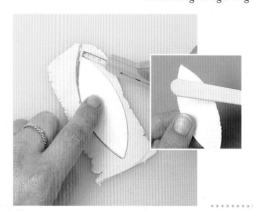

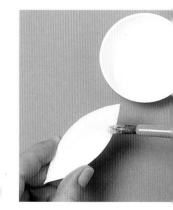

Apply a smooth paste to the clay with your fingers to fill any fine cracks and surface dents. Let dry completely.

5. Paint both sides and edges of the shape white. Let dry (read paint instructions for drying time—the paint might still be tacky to the touch even when it appears dry).

6.

Lightly outline your design in pencil.

7.

Use blue paints to complete the design, let them dry, and then fire in the oven following the clay package instructions. Glue a pin back in place to complete.

Variations on a Theme

A star-shaped cookie cutter and vivid acrylic paints were used to create this dazzling pin (right).

A tiny circular cookie cutter was used to create this mini plate pin. Simple brush strokes used for the flower petals add to the feel of hand-painted pottery (far right).

Stick Pins & Hat PINS

Some of the first stick pins were those worn by people in ancient civilizations to hold their clothes together before sewing or buttons were invented. Elaborate beaded pins were frequently worn, and the more powerful the person, the more ornate were the designs. Today hat and lapel pins are largely decorative and are a great way of adding your own personal stamp to an outfit.

Hat pins can be used to totally transform a simple hat into a glamorous, expensive-looking hat, especially if it's decorated with fabulous feather plumes or an ornate collection of beads. These pins don't have to be confined to hats—they look wonderful worn on a lapel and are a perfect way to add a touch of style to a plain outfit. Shorter versions look striking as scarf pins. Pins are available with protective caps for the pointed tips from jewelry and craft suppliers and come in a variety of lengths to suit different needs. Some come with flat discs at the top, which you can decorate with all kinds of materials from traditional beads and jewel stones to jeweler's wire, feathers, and modeling clay. Feathers can be bought in every color imaginable and even dyed to match a special outfit. Natural feathers like peacock and pheasant are appealing on felt hats in muted country colors. They can be attached to the top of pins with matching thread or inserted into complementary beads or even shank-backed buttons. Jeweler's wire in thicker gauges can be shaped into coils and decorated with beads or jewel stones for a totally modern look, and modeling clay helps re-create ideas inspired by the past.

Beaded Metal
SWIRLS

Design Tips

Choose a pin to suit the use of the design—lapel pins are shorter than hat pins.

Experiment by bending jeweler's wire around different shapes to create a variety of designs.

The wire can also be hammered into shape to create a completely different effect—use thicker wires and a rawhide hammer or an ordinary hammer covered with a piece of suede or felt.

Look for unusual feathers—perhaps from an unused feather duster.

Beads with large holes can be slipped on after the wire has been shaped and glued to secure, or you can try beading the wire first and then carefully shaping it for a more ornate finish.

OGETHER WITH BEADS, JEWELER'S WIRE RATES AS one of the most essential and versatile materials to have in your craft jewelry box. It comes in a variety of thicknesses and colors—real gold, silver, and copper, plus plated alternatives that are less expensive. The wire can be used to make your own basic findings or for more decorative work like these contemporary pins. The metal is soft enough to be shaped into intricate designs using a variety of objects as basic forms, from pliers to pieces of wood. The finished piece can then be attached to a purchased stick pin or to one made from the same metal and filed to a point at one end. Decorated with jewels or beads, the finished pins can be designed to coordinate with a favorite hat or outfit.

Getting Started

This piece requires jeweler's wire, about 0.05 inch / 1.2 mm thick for the metal swirls, and 0.03 inch / 0.8 mm thick for binding the metal swirls to the stick pin.

BEADED METAL SWIRLS

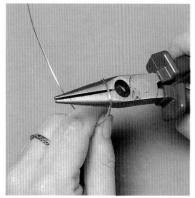

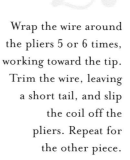

1. Cut 2 pieces of thick wire, each 10 inches / 25.5 cm long, and grip one end with the widest end of the pliers.

2. Wrap the wire around the pliers 5 or 6 times, working toward the tip. Trim the wire, leaving a short tail, and slip the coil off the pliers. Repeat for the other piece.

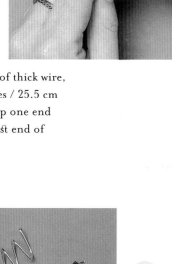

3. Holding the widest end of the coil with your fingers and the other end with the pliers, gently stretch out the coil. Straighten the tail at the narrowest point with pliers.

4. Trim the end of the first wrap to approximately ¼ inch / 0.5 cm.

5. Place the top of the stick pin between the 2 tails left at the narrower ends of the coils and bind them together tightly with fine wire. Wrap the wire evenly and trim when the joint feels totally secure.

6. Straighten out the tips at the other end enough to slip on the beads. Add as many beads as you want, slipping them over the coils toward the center but leaving them spaced out. Fold the tips of the wire back on themselves to form hooks and glue the beads securely.

7. The beads in the center can be glued or left loose for an interesting effect.

Variations on a Theme

This single coil was shaped over a wooden dowel, decorated with pearls and black beads, joined to a disc-topped lapel pin, and then decorated with a coordinating flat-backed jewel stone (right).

Here copper wire has been worked into flat spirals and the centers decorated with jewel stones (far right). Try making your own pin from wire cut and shaped to a point.

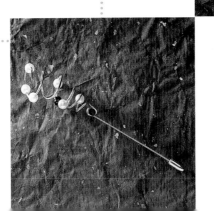

Jazzy Jeweled
PIN

Design Tips

Sketch out your design on paper and work out the color scheme and decoration before starting on the real thing.

Experiment with different types of paints, paint techniques, and design ideas.

For glitzy, ornate designs, use metallic paints and bright, faceted jewel stones; for a more natural feel, experiment with stone-finish textured paints and natural, smooth, flat-backed mineral stones.

Layer the papier-mâché carefully for a smooth finished surface and paint with a detailed design using acrylic or gouache paint.

Once you have mastered the basic principles, you can use different types of paper as a finishing layer instead of paint. Handmade paper, decorative foil, and even wrapping paper can be used as a final layer and then simply finished with a few coats of varnish.

THE BASE FOR THIS FUN ABSTRACT PIN WAS MADE BY layering pasted strips of newspaper over a shape cut from thick cardboard. It shows how versatile the craft of papier-mâché is; by working with very narrow strips of paper, you can cover the most intricate shapes to give them a strong, sturdy finish. In the past, craftspeople used these techniques to make tables and chairs, and in Scandinavia an entire church was built from papier-mâché! Traditionally the paper is carefully placed in even layers to create a smooth finished surface, but interesting textured finishes can be achieved by layering the paper more randomly. This then provides the perfect base for decorative paint and allows you to let your imagination run free with ideas for different finished effects. For detailed directions on making perfect papier-mâché, refer to the Golden Celtic Shield project.

Cardboard
Pencil
Scissors
Wallpaper paste
Paste brush
Small strips of torn newspaper
PVA glue
Gesso
Paintbrush
Gold metallic Plaka paint
Small block of plasticine
Several colorful flat-backed jewel stones
Tweezers
All-purpose, clear-drying glue
Stick pin with disc top and protective cap

Getting Started

This simple papier-mâché project involves pasting small strips of newspaper over a cardboard shape that is then painted with gesso and acrylic paint. Follow the package instructions to make a small amount of wallpaper paste.

JAZZY JEWELED PIN

Draw your shape on
thick cardboard freehand
or with tracing paper.
Cut it out carefully using
sharp scissors.

Apply paste to a strip
of newspaper and place
it on one side of the
shape so that a little
extends beyond the
edge. Smooth it flat
with your fingers.

Smooth the protruding
end over to the opposite
side, making sure the edge
is smooth. Continue
layering pasted strips
over the shape, covering
both sides and the edges.
You will need 4 to 6 layers
in all to create a firm,
finished piece, and the
last 2 or 3 should be
painted with PVA glue
instead of paste to give a
more durable finish. Let
dry completely.

Paint with artist's
gesso. This acts as an
undercoat and prevents
the newsprint from
showing through the
painted finish.

5.

Glue the pin in place at the base of the shape—this gives you something to hold when painting.

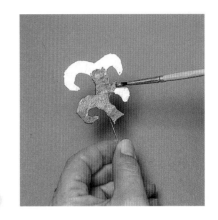

6.

Paint both sides and the edges of the shape gold. Let dry and add another coat if necessary.

7.

Insert the point of the pin onto a block of plasticine to hold it flat and then cover it with jewel stones placed at random but highlighting the shape of the finished design.

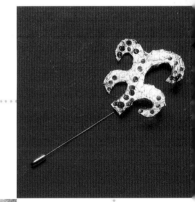

Variations on a Theme

The same shape has been painted in rich purple; textured glitter paints add a decorative finish instead of jewel stones (right).

Liquid beads are another way of adding a decorative finish. They can be used to create an abstract pattern of their own or placed in a more regular design (far right).

Bronzed
HEART

TODAY'S SYNTHETIC CLAYS PROVIDE THE CRAFT jeweler with an ideal modeling medium to create a wealth of different shapes. You might be inspired by traditional fine jewelry designs; with practice the clay can be molded and sculpted to resemble the intricate shapes usually worked in precious metals. Or you can choose sleeker, more modern shapes and use decorative beads to add an ornate finish. A range of different clays are available, from the colorful polymer varieties to the more traditional-looking air-dry types available in simple plaster or terra-cotta finishes. For this design you can use either type, and it is a great way of utilizing small leftover pieces. The idea was inspired by a book on jewelry design and could be worked into an infinite variety of shapes.

You Will Need

Polymer clay
2 round cookie cutters
Stick pin with protective cap
Polymer clay varnish
Bronze powder
Toothpick or wooden skewer
Paintbrush
Decorative bronze beads
All-purpose clear-drying glue
Small rolling pin

Getting Started

Thoroughly knead a small amount of polymer clay to soften and remove air bubbles. Obtain 2 round cookie cutters—one approximately 2 inches / 5 cm in diameter, the other 1 inch / 2.5 cm in diameter.

BRONZED HEART

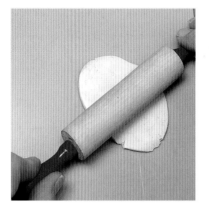

1.

Roll out the clay to a depth of approximately ¼ inch / 0.5 cm.

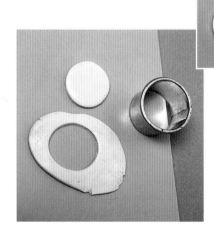

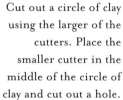

2.

Cut out a circle of clay using the larger of the cutters. Place the smaller cutter in the middle of the circle of clay and cut out a hole.

3.

Carefully insert the pin through the clay, making sure it is centered.

4.

Gently pull the pin so that the blunt end rests on the outer edge of the clay, puckering it slightly to create a stylized heart shape. Fire in a low-temperature oven following the clay package instructions, leaving the pin in place. Let cool completely.

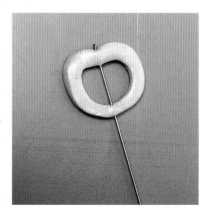

5.

Place a little varnish in a dish and sprinkle on the bronze powder. Mix together with a tooth-pick or wooden skewer, making sure the powder is completely dispersed. Add as much as you need to create the right depth of color.

6.

Paint all surfaces of the heart, making sure not to get any on the wire.

7.

Carefully remove the pin and thread on the first bead. Insert the tip of the pin back through the hole, adding another bead so that it falls in the center of the heart. Push the pin out the hole on the opposite side and add the final bead. Glue this in place to secure.

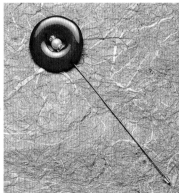

Variations on a Theme

Heart-shaped cutters of different sizes were used to make this simple design, which was then glued to a disc-topped stick pin (right).

A different effect can be produced with a doughnut bead that has been beaded and glued in place. Glue the beads to the pin so that they fall in the central hole (far right).

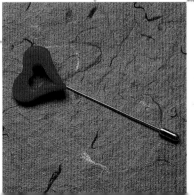

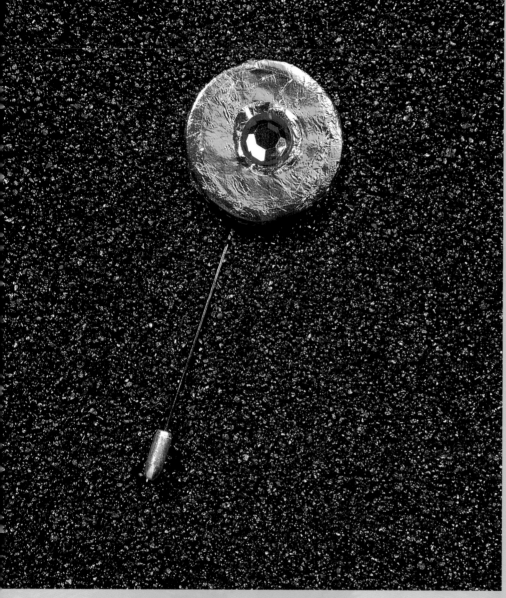

Foil MAGIC

Design Tips

Experiment with different base shapes, using cookie cutters or cardboard templates.

Sketch different design ideas on paper, first working out the size and shape of foil papers needed.

Experiment with different color combinations and, if working more intricate designs, practice on paper first to ensure a perfect finish.

To add pattern as well as color to the pin, substitute decorative paper for the foil papers.

Gummed foil shapes made for children's crafts can also create great effects.

Use artist's mat board instead of polymer clay to create the base shape of the pin.

A SIMPLE BASE SHAPE FROM CLAY OR PAPIER-

mâché can be given a dazzling finish with

brightly colored foil papers used to

wrap chocolates and other candy. Before you throw away

a wrapper, check whether it can be incorporated into a

stunning piece of jewelry. You can use the foil to create

simple designs like this one or have fun working more intricate

patterns with different colors cut into smaller shapes to give

the impression of a mosaic. Outlined in gold or decorated with

coordinating jewels, the finished effect is spectacular. These foil

wrappers come in fabulous jewel-like colors and are perfect for

making jazzy jewelry. At certain times of the year, like Easter and

Christmas, you can find wrappers with wonderful decorative

patterns that create spectacular effects.

Getting Started

To avoid wasting foil, work out the size and color of each circle on
scrap paper or cardboard before you cut the foil. For this project, you
will need to cut out 3 circles of foil in one color: one that is slightly
larger than the finished design (to allow for turning the edges to the
reverse side); another in the exact same size (to use as backing); and a
third, smaller circle for the center. Cut out a fourth, medium-sized
circle in a contrasting color.

You Will Need

Polymer clay
Round 2-inch / 5 cm cookie cutter
Cardboard
Compass
Pencil
Colored foil candy wrappers
Scissors
All-purpose, clear-drying glue
Flat-backed jewel stone
Tweezers
Disc-topped stick pin
with protective cap

FOIL MAGIC

1. To work out the size of each piece of foil, draw a circle 2 inches / 5 cm in diameter on cardboard by drawing around the circumference of a round cookie cutter or by using a compass. Draw a ⅜ inch / 1 cm border outside this circle to allow for turning the edge of the foil over to the wrong side of the clay base. Next, draw 2 smaller circles within the main outline, each slightly smaller than the previous one.

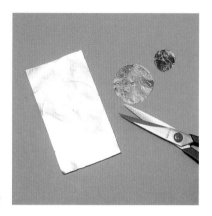

2. Using the card pattern as a size guide and a compass to draw the outlines, cut out 3 circles of foil in the main color and a fourth circle in a contrasting foil color as outlined in Getting Started and in step 1.

3. Knead a small amount of clay thoroughly to soften and remove air bubbles and roll out to a depth of approximately ¼ inch / 0.5 cm. Use the cookie cutter to cut out the main shape and fire it in a low-temperature oven, following clay package instructions.

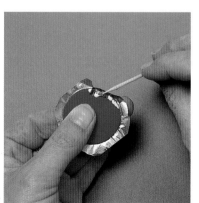

4. When the clay is cool, place the largest circle of foil over the clay shape, clip the curved edges, and glue it to the opposite side, using a toothpick to smooth the foil over the edge.

5.

Glue the backing circle over the top to conceal the edges and let dry.

6.

Position the contrasting circle of foil centrally on the front of the pin and glue to secure. Let dry. Add the last foil circle in the same way, then glue a jewel stone to the center.

7.

Glue the stick pin in position to complete the pin.

Variations on a Theme

Colorful patterned paper from a chocolate Easter egg was used to make this fun variation on the same theme (right).

A totally different effect was achieved with a foil cup that had been used to contain a chocolate. The foil was washed, flattened, and finished with a bold central jewel (far right).

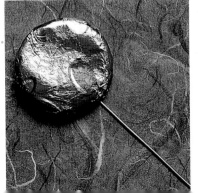

Marble & Pearl
PIN

Design Tips

To get the best finish from polymer modeling clays, knead well to soften and remove any air bubbles. This should then create a smooth surface when the clay is rolled out.

Leaving the clay wrapped in a plastic bag on top of a towel on a warm radiator helps speed up the softening time, especially on old clay. Alternatively, you can buy special preparations produced by the manufacturer that do the same job.

Practice getting the perfect marbled effect by working with small pieces of clay before beginning the actual project.

When you've mastered the technique of marbling, you can move on to experiment with more extensive color combinations.

Books on the history of jewelry and the styles of different periods can provide great inspiration for different shapes.

T HE INSPIRATION FOR THIS UNUSUAL PIN DESIGN COMES from the strong shapes that were fashionable during the Art Deco period. The design idea is then reworked in malleable polymer clay that comes in a wide range of colors and looks wonderful blended together to create dramatic marbled effects. You can use any color combination you like to create marbled effects—with practice it is even possible to create a blend that mimics real precious stones such as lapis lazuli or malachite. The blended clay can be rolled out like pastry dough and cut into shapes with cookie cutters or a cardboard template and craft knife. Two different shapes gently pressed together will fuse when fired in a low-temperature oven. By attaching a finding to the soft clay, you can also hang charm drops for additional decoration.

You Will Need

Polymer clay in 2 colors
Rolling pin
Circular cookie cutters
or cardboard templates
Craft knife
Ruler
4 eye pins
Wire cutters
All-purpose, clear-drying glue
Varnish
2 jump rings
2 pearl drop beads
Pliers
Stick pin with disc top
and protective cap

Getting Started

Knead the Fimo with your thumbs and fingers until soft and pliable—this will prevent cracks and make it much easier to roll. Wash your hands when changing colors to prevent one color from mixing into another and spoiling the finished effect. Use 2 different cookie cutters or cardboard templates, 2 inches / 5 cm and 1 inch / 2.5 cm in diameter, to create the circular discs.

MARBLE & PEARL PIN

Roll out a log of Fimo in each color. Wrap these around one another and roll to form a single log. Fold this in half, twist the 2 halves together, and knead to blend the colors. Continue twisting and kneading until you have the desired marbled effect.

Roll the clay out like pastry dough to a depth of approximately ¼ inch / 0.5 cm.

Cut out a circle of marbled clay 1 inch / 2.5 cm in diameter, using the smaller cutter.

Select one of the colors used for marbling and roll out as before. Cut out a circle with the larger cutter and then position the smaller cutter on top, close to one edge. Cut out the smaller circle and discard. Using a ruler and craft knife, trim the shape as shown.

5. Butt this crescent shape up against the marbled circle and gently smooth the joining edges. Trim 2 eye pins to about ⅜ inch / 1 cm and insert into the clay as shown. Fire in a low-temperature oven following package instructions.

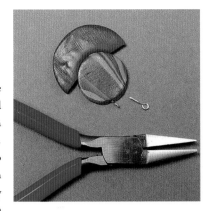

6. Add a dab of glue to secure the eye pins inserted in the clay. Varnish it to bring out the colors in the clay. Slip the pearl drops onto the eye pins, trim the wire to within ⅜ inch / 1 cm of the bead top, and make a loop with the pliers. Slip open jump rings through the loops of the beaded pins and the pins in the clay. Close to secure.

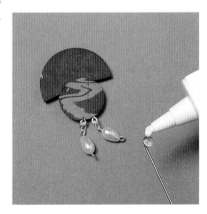

7. Glue a stick pin in place to complete the design.

Variations on a Theme

The same idea has been adapted in plain clays to create a different shape. This time the design is finished with a central jewel stone and a coordinating glass bead drop (right).

Place several crescents of clay side by side in alternating colors and finish with a small circle of clay for another variation on the same theme (far right).

Links, Drops, & Bar
PINS

y linking charm drops or using unusual materials you can create much more elaborate pins than the traditional stick or badge styles. These styles can be fixed to any pin finding and fastened to a coat, blouse, scarf, or hat. Look for different materials—such as pretty ribbons, wire mesh, and even shells—to create totally original designs.

Modeling clay can be shaped with cookie cutters and given textured finishes using all kinds of different objects, or it can be cut into more definite forms like starfish and decorated with pretty shell dangles. Wire mesh is pliable enough to be worked into simple or complex shapes and can be decorated with dazzling jewel stones or "found" objects such as charms from broken necklaces or bracelets. Make pretty fabrics rigid by using fabric stiffening products or simple PVA glue. This gives the fabric form and allows you to create permanent pleats and gathers. Special perforated findings can be bought with claws to clamp over corresponding pin backs, and these can be embroidered with small beads and even buttons. Pierced backs are also perfect for sewing fabric pins to because they are often difficult to join successfully to flat surfaces. Pin backs like these, together with plain metal discs and ovals, are available from jewelry, bead, and craft suppliers.

Jeweled Lace
ROSETTE

Experiment with different types of fabric—ribbons are ideal, since their edges are already neatened, but you can also use strips of any fabric.

Apply the PVA to a scrap piece of fabric first to see how many coats will be required to get the rigidity you desire.

PVA gives some fabrics an obvious shine. Do a test piece to make sure you are happy with the finish.

Experiment with different pin shapes by pleating or folding the fabric origami-style rather than just using a plain circle.

You can also achieve different effects by first painting or embroidering the fabric. The colors of some embroidery threads can run, so first paint a small piece with PVA to test it.

T HE USE OF FABRIC IN JEWELRY DESIGN IS BECOMING increasingly popular and offers limitless opportunities for innovative ideas. Nothing is impossible when creating this kind of "soft" jewelry—let your imagination run wild. Even traditional crafts such as embroidery, quilting, and patchwork can be applied to jewelry designs. Stiffening fabric with PVA glue gives it another dimension, as this rosette pin illustrates. It is made from a length of pretty lace edging that has been gathered at one edge to create the rosette effect and then painted with PVA. The PVA gives the fabric a clear, nearly invisible, plastic-like coating that helps keep it rigid and in shape. (You can also buy prepared solutions for stiffening fabrics from craft suppliers.) Lace comes with ready-made holes that are perfect for linking charms, and the stiffened finish will prevent it from tearing. The pretty drop for this pin was taken from a broken earring, but you could easily make your own.

Getting Started

Look for lace edging with a repeating floral or figure design that is approximately 1 inch / 2.5 cm wide. Rummage around your bead or sewing box for colored glass beads, a single bead drop from a broken earring, and a single pearl bead (for the center).

You Will Need

Strip of lace edging
Scissors
Matching heavy thread
Needle
PVA glue
Paintbrush
A bead drop from a broken earring
or 2 pearl drop beads
and 2 colored glass beads
Pearl bead for the center
Jump ring
Pliers
Pin back

JEWELED LACE ROSETTE

1.

Cut a strip of lace
10 inches / 25.5 cm
long.

2.

Fold under the cut edge
of one of the short ends
of the lace and press
with a cool iron. Layer
this end over the other
short end to form a
circle. Slip-stitch to
hold in place.

3.

Make a knot in one
end of a piece of thread.
Sew a row of long
running stitches along
the bottom edge of the
lace circle.

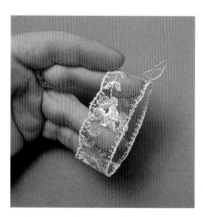

4.

Pull the thread up so
that the lace forms a
rosette shape.

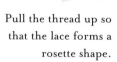

5.

With the needle still threaded, stitch through the center of the gathered lace to secure.

6.

Carefully paint the rosette with a light coat of PVA glue and let dry. Add another coat if required.

7.

To finish, glue or sew a pearl to the center point of the rosette. Slip a jump ring through the lace near one edge and then add the bead charm, closing the jump ring to secure. Sew or glue to a pin back.

Variations on a Theme

Here the same idea has been worked with a pretty chiffon ribbon. This time the fabric has been stiffened with hairspray to make a pin in an instant and, since the fabric is too fine to add a drop to, a dramatic jewel stone adds decorative interest at the center (right).

A finely pleated ribbon rosette makes a sensational pin that could be worn on a lapel or used to decorate a hat (far right).

Textured
EFFECTS

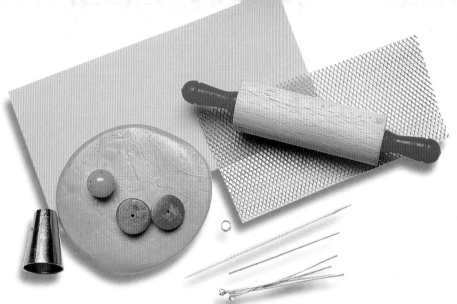

P ERFECTLY SMOOTH, even surfaces are ideal for painting and decorating in all manners, but you can also have fun adding texture. This is simple to do on synthetic clays before they are fired, because the surface is receptive to anything pressed onto it. You can use an endless variety of objects—this project and the variations shown used a piece of wire mesh, a nutmeg grater, and a shell. You could also try a cheese grater, string, coins—anything that has an interesting textured finish. Textural effects can also be achieved by adding relief details using additional clay in the same color or in contrasting colors. Small pieces of clay are easy to add to the surface and will fuse when fired in a low-temperature oven.

Getting Started

To gauge how much pressure is needed to get a clean, textured finish, practice pressing the wire mesh or sieve into spare pieces of clay.

You Will Need

Block of polymer clay
Cardboard
Pencil
Compass
Rolling pin
Craft knife
Top of a piping bag or similar round "cutter"
Toothpick
Wire mesh (or metal sieve)
Several beads to coordinate with color of clay
4 eye pins
Straight pin
Wire cutters
Jump ring
Pliers
Pin back
All-purpose, clear-drying glue

TEXTURED EFFECTS

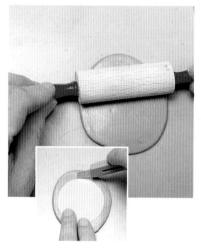

1. Knead the clay until warm and pliable, then roll out like pastry dough on a flat surface to a depth of about ⅜ inch / 1 cm. Draw a circle, 3 inches / 7.5 cm in diameter, on a piece of cardboard and cut it out. Place the circle on the clay and cut it out carefully with a craft knife.

2. Use the top from a piping bag to cut out a central circle, forming a doughnut-like shape.

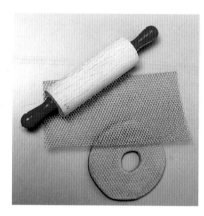

3. Pierce a hole from the outside edge to the center with a toothpick.

4. Place the piece of wire mesh or a kitchen sieve over the surface of the doughnut and press down firmly (use the rolling pin if working with mesh).

5. Use the toothpick to draw lines in the clay that radiate out from the center. Then fire in a low-temperature oven following clay package instructions.

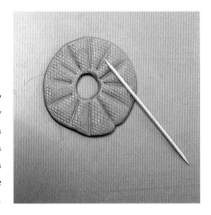

6. Using pliers, make a spiral from an eye pin working up the wire from the opposite end to the eye.

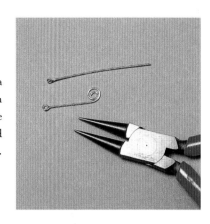

7. Push a head pin through the hole already made in the pin base, inserting it from the center of the doughnut shape. Turn a loop in the protruding end. Make the charm drop by linking together a group of beads and a single bead wired with eye pins. Add the metal spiral to the last bead, and join the charm to the loop on the pin base using a jump ring. Finish by gluing a pin back to the wrong side.

Variations on a Theme

For this pin, texture has been added by pressing a metal nutmeg grater into the surface (right).

This pin looks like a piece of ancient sculpture, but the design was created by pressing a shell into stone-imitation polymer clay (far right).

Starfish &
SEASHELLS PIN

THIS PRETTY PIN WAS INSPIRED BY A visit to the seashore and uses tiny, perfectly formed shells as charm drops. By drilling small holes in larger shells, you can link several together to make variations on the same theme. The starfish is easy to make from polymer or air-dry clays, but if you are lucky enough to find a real one of the right size, you can drill holes in two of the arms and join shell drops in the same way. To find a motif to use for a cardboard template, look at rubber stamps or books on shells and the sea. Children's books are often the best because they usually have simple, clearly defined illustrations that are easy to trace off the page. You can buy shells from specialist suppliers, but there is nothing more rewarding than using those you've found yourself.

Getting Started

Select 4 tiny shells of similar color and size to create a balanced finished effect. Shells this small will shatter if drilled, so to join them together you will need to glue eye pins trimmed in size to the reverse side of each shell.

You Will Need

Block of polymer clay
Cardboard
Pencil
Rolling pin
Craft knife
Toothpick
4 small seashells
4 eye pins
Wire cutters
All-purpose clear-drying glue
2 large jump ring
2 small jump rings
Pliers
Pin back

STARFISH & SEASHELLS PIN

1. Draw the starfish motif on cardboard and cut it out carefully, getting into all the angles.

2. Knead the clay until warm and pliable and roll out like pastry dough on a flat surface to a depth of about ⅜ inch / 1 cm.

3. Place the cardboard star on the clay and cut out the shape with a craft knife. Smooth the edges carefully and pierce a hole with a toothpick in 2 adjacent arms. Fire in a low-temperature oven according to the clay package instructions.

4. Trim eye pins to fit the shell so that the eye of the pin just extends out from the shell. The shell nearest the starfish will need another loop as well as the eye of the pin (so it can be joined to the starfish and the second shell), but the second shell requires only one loop.

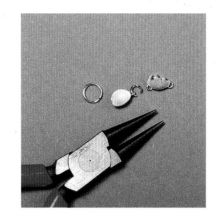

Grasping the shells firmly with tweezers, glue the eye pins in place. Hold until the glue begins to set to ensure that the pins stay in position.

6.

Using pliers, twist open a small jump ring and slip it through the loops on both shells. Close the ring again to secure.

7.

Twist open a large jump ring and push it through the hole in one arm of the starfish and through the loop of the top shell. Close to secure. Repeat for the other side and finish by gluing a pin back in place on the reverse side.

Variations on a Theme

Pretty shells linked together with jump rings make unusual pins. Pad out the concave back of the shell with paper pulp or plaster to provide a base for the pin back (right).

Look for interesting shell shapes like this long golden shell with pretty spiral markings to use on its own or to link to other shells (far right).

Glittering
METAL MESH

Design Tips

Experiment with different shapes and decorative finishes. Templates can be drawn with a dark china marker, which will rub off.

You can file raw edges smooth, turn them to the wrong side with pliers, or paint them with PVA glue.

Try folding or pleating the metal to get interesting effects, using a steel ruler or the edge of a pair of pliers to press against. Wear protective gloves to prevent the metal from scratching your hands.

Treat the mesh like canvas and embroider with tiny beads and beading wire.

You can use heavy-duty tin cutters to cut more ornate pierced metals.

CRAFT STORES THAT SPECIALIZE IN SUPPLYING sculptors are a haven for innovative jewelry designers because they carry a wide range of different materials that you can use to create exciting, original designs. Pliable wire mesh is usually used as a base for applying plaster, but, dressed up with crystal jewel stones and an ornate metal spiral, it can be transformed into a chic, modern pin. It is soft enough to be cut into strips and wrapped around a pencil or wooden dowel to make curved shapes or can be folded or pleated for more interesting effects. You are advised to wear protective gloves when cutting, since the metal has sharp edges that can scratch the skin. If you are cutting out intricate shapes, wear goggles to prevent small pieces from flying into your eyes.

Getting Started

Jeweler's wire is usually sold on spools. For this project, you will need wire that is 0.05 inch / 1.2 mm thick.

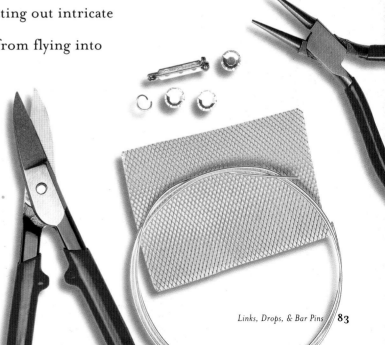

You Will Need

Small piece of wire mesh
(usually bought in rolls)
Steel ruler
Tin cutters or heavy-duty
household scissors
Straight pin
Block of polystyrene, foam,
or plasticine
Flat-backed jewel stones
Jeweler's wire
Round-nosed pliers
Jump ring
All-purpose, clear-drying glue
Pin back

GLITTERING METAL MESH

1. Cut a narrow strip of mesh from the roll. Measure and mark a square 1½ inches / 4 cm on each side.

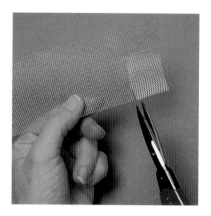

2. Cut out the square using the pattern of the mesh to keep the lines straight.

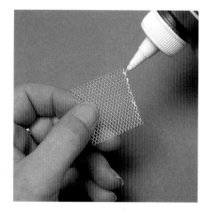

3. Apply a narrow border of PVA glue to cover the raw edges. (Or, as an alternative, smooth the edges with a fine metal file.)

4. To dry the mesh without accidentally gluing it to a surface, suspend it on a pin inserted in a block of polystyrene, foam, or plasticine.

5.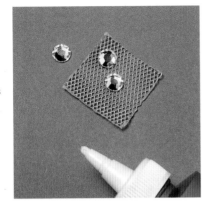

Arrange jewel stones and glue into position.

6.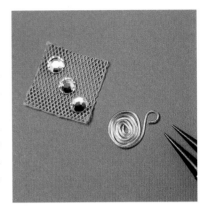

Cut a piece of jeweler's wire 6 inches / 15 cm long. Using round-nosed pliers, make a loop in one end of the wire and then make a spiral by working up from the opposite end.

7.

Twist open a jump ring, slip it through a hole close to a corner of the mesh square and through the loop at the top of the metal spiral. Close to secure. Glue the pin back to the reverse side, positioning it behind the jewel stones so it won't show through the mesh.

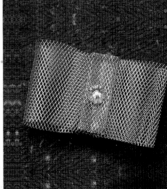

Variations on a Theme

By curving the edges and gluing a metal spiral taken from a broken necklace to the center, the same idea is given a new look (right).

By folding and shaping the metal, you can make more stylized shapes (far right). The center bead is held in place with a head pin, which was twisted into a spiral on the back.

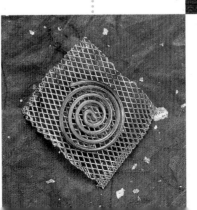

Experiment with the variety of different-shaped punches available —look for hearts, teddy bears, birds, butterflies, and more from craft specialists.

Artist's mat board is perfect for making brooch bases. Try cutting out different shapes—ovals, oblongs, hearts, flowers, circles, and triangles are easy, but you could also experiment with more abstract shapes.

If you can't find neoprene, sequins are a great substitute and can be used to create more glamorous finished pieces.

Tiny flat-backed jewel stones can also be used to create dazzling effects.

Paint the cardboard different colors to vary the background or buy colored mount board.

Pop-Art
PIN

N EOPRENE IS AN EXCITING ADDITION to the wide range of craft materials currently available. It has a wonderfully tactile finish that is like soft rubber and fascinates adults and children alike. It is extremely versatile and can be used to create flat motifs as well as three-dimensional shapes—it can even be used to make chunky, rolled beads in the same way as paper. Available from craft specialists in sheet form or pre-cut shapes like flowers, hearts, and circles, it comes in a wide range of colors. You can draw shapes on it easily and cut out intricate details with scissors or a craft knife. For this design, a single hole punch was used to cut out tiny circles, which were then glued to a cardboard base in a pattern and colors inspired by Pop Art designs of the 1960s.

Getting Started

Tweezers are useful for picking up the tiny neoprene circles, which should be placed so that they just touch each other. A toothpick will help you position the circles exactly.

You Will Need

Neoprene in 3 different colors (red, orange, and yellow suit the theme)
Ruler
Pencil
Small piece of mat board or thick cardboard
Craft knife or scissors
Single-hole punch
All-purpose, clear-drying glue
Tweezers
Toothpick
Acrylic paint
Paintbrush
Pin back

POP-ART PIN

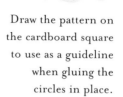

Draw the pattern on the cardboard square to use as a guideline when gluing the circles in place.

Draw a square, 1¾ inches / 4.5 cm, on the mat board and cut it out using a craft knife or sharp scissors.

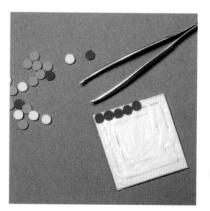

Use the hole punch to cut out tiny circles from each of the different-colored pieces of neo-prene—approximately 30 red, 20 orange, and 16 yellow.

Apply glue to the surface of the cardboard and start the first horizontal line of circles.

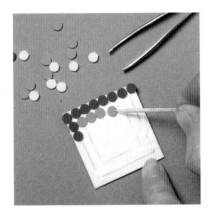

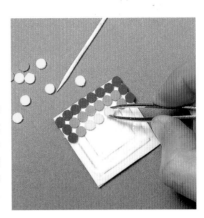

Start the vertical line to help set the pattern, then add the next color.

Glue the rest of the circles in place, working in lines from top to bottom and adding more glue if it begins to dry out.

Paint the back and sides of the square in a coordinating color. When the paint is dry, complete the design by gluing a pin back in position.

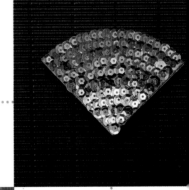

Variations on a Theme

Tiny beads in jazzy colors glued to a simple base shape create a dazzling pin (right).

A pretty fan shape has been created by cutting out a rounded triangle from mat board and covering with sequins in several shades of the same color (far right).

Acknowledgments

Grateful thanks to the many people without whose help and support this book would not have been published. First and most important, to my parents for their endless patience and for turning a blind eye when I used their home as a design studio. To Lindsey Stock and Jackie Schou for their additional design ideas, and to Paul Forrester for his creative photography. And, finally, to Shawna Mullen and Martha Wetherill, who made sense of everything I have written and gave valuable support and encouragement when times got tough.

About the Author

Jo Moody is a journalist who specializes in fashion and craft, and who has spent many years working for women's magazines. She is now a freelance stylist and writer, contributing features and designs to a variety of publications. Her childhood fascination with jewelry has developed into a passion—she loves rediscovering traditional crafts and using them in new ways to transform everyday things into truly beautiful jewelry.

Index

Sketch your ideas ...